THE
MAGIC WITHIN

A GUIDED JOURNAL

DANICA GIM

THOUGHT
CATALOG
Books

THOUGHTCATALOG.COM
NEW YORK · LOS ANGELES

THOUGHT
CATALOG
Books

Published by Thought Catalog Books, an im-
print of the digital magazine Thought Catalog,
which is owned and operated by The Thought
& Expression Company LLC, an independent
media organization based in Brooklyn, New
York and Los Angeles, California.

Made in the USA.

ISBN 978-1-949759-35-8

This book was produced by Chris Lavergne
and Noelle Beams. Layout by KJ Parish. Special
thanks to Brianna Wiest for creative editorial
direction and Isidoros Karamitopoulos for
circulation management.

Visit us on the web at thoughtcatalog.com and
shopcatalog.com.

HEY YOU!

I'M SO EXCITED YOU ARE HOLDING THIS BOOK!
WHETHER YOU ARE AN EXPERIENCED JOURNALER
OR JUST GETTING STARTED,
I DESIGNED THIS GUIDED JOURNAL TO CREATE A UNIQUE,
FUN AND HELPFUL EXPERIENCE ESPECIALLY FOR YOU!
DID YOU KNOW THAT 21 DAYS IS ENOUGH TO
CREATE A NEW HABIT AND TO REWIRE YOUR
BRAIN TO BE MORE POSITIVE?
THAT'S RIGHT! THAT'S ALL IT TAKES!
THAT'S WHY THIS JOURNAL INCLUDES 21 SECTIONS
THAT WILL INSPIRE YOU TO WRITE EACH DAY.

OF COURSE, YOU ARE FREE TO EXTEND THE 21 DAY
PERIOD TO HOWEVER LONG YOU NEED TO
COMPLETE THE EXERCISES. IF YOU FIND
YOURSELF NEEDING MORE SPACE FOR WRITING,
THE LAST PART OF THIS BOOK IS FILLED WITH EXTRA
BLANK PAGES! I HOPE YOU ENJOY YOUR JOURNEY HERE!

X DANICA ♡

DAILY REMINDER

YOU ARE EXACTLY
WHERE YOU NEED
TO BE.

WHICH EMOTIONS ARE YOU FEELING TODAY?

grateful, lonely, determined, positive, aware

WHICH PHYSICAL SENSATIONS ARE YOU FEELING TODAY?

DID YOU KNOW THAT STUDIES HAVE SHOWN THAT LISTING THREE THINGS YOU ARE GRATEFUL FOR ON A DAILY BASIS INCREASES YOUR HEALTH AND HAPPINESS? YOUR SOURCES OF GRATITUDE DON'T NEED TO BE COMPLEX. EVEN A GOOD CUP OF COFFEE CAN MAKE THE LIST. IT WILL HAVE A MORE PROFOUND EFFECT IF YOU WRITE DOWN WHY YOU ARE GRATEFUL FOR THESE THINGS AS WELL.

DAILY GRATITUDE

1.

2.

3.

USE THE NEXT PAGE FOR JOURNALING

WHAT IS CURRENTLY MAKING ME HAPPY?

WHAT SURPRISED ME TODAY?

WHAT DO I WANT TO DO DIFFERENTLY TOMORROW?

DAILY
REMINDER

REMEMBER THAT YOU ARE THE SOURCE OF YOUR OWN POWER.

WHICH EMOTIONS ARE
YOU FEELING TODAY ?

WHICH PHYSICAL
SENSATIONS ARE YOU
FEELING TODAY ?

DAILY GRATITUDE

1.

2.

3.

AFFIRMATIONS

AFFIRMATIONS ARE SHORT, SIMPLE, AND, POWERFUL EXPRESSIONS. BY FIRMLY DECLARING A POSITIVE THOUGHT, THESE SENTENCES ARE AIMED TO AFFECT THE CONSCIOUS AND SUBCONSCIOUS MIND SO THAT OUR HABITS, BEHAVIOR, AND THINKING PATTERNS ARE ALTERED IN A POSITIVE WAY.

AFFIRMATIONS HAVE A PROFOUND EFFECT
ON OUR THOUGHT PATTERNS AND CAN HELP
MAKE YOU FEEL MORE POSITIVE,
EMPOWERED, AND GRATEFUL.
OUR MIND IS POWERFUL AND IT WILL LISTEN
TO THE MESSAGES WE ARE PROGRAMMING INTO IT.

AFFIRMATION TIPS

START WITH "I AM"

USE PRESENT TENSE

STATE THE POSITIVE
(AFFIRM WHAT YOU WANT, NOT WHAT YOU DON'T WANT)

EXAMPLES OF AFFIRMING FEELINGS

I AM SO LOVED

I AM FULL OF ENERGY

I AM ABLE AND CONFIDENT

EXAMPLES OF AFFIRMING EVENTS

I AM CELEBRATING GRADUATING FROM COLLEGE

I AM CONFIDENTLY ACCEPTING MY DREAM JOB

DAILY GRATITUDE

1.

2.

3.

USE THE NEXT PAGE
FOR JOURNALING

SOME HELPFUL QUESTIONS

WHAT AM I
PROUD OF TODAY?

WHAT WENT
WELL TODAY?

WHAT COULD
I HAVE DONE
BETTER?

DAILY
REMINDER

DARLING, YOU HAVE ALWAYS
BEEN MAGIC

WHICH EMOTIONS ARE
YOU FEELING TODAY ?

WHICH PHYSICAL
SENSATIONS ARE YOU
FEELING TODAY ?

DAILY GRATITUDE

1.

2.

3.

BRAIN DRAIN

THE GOAL OF "BRAIN DRAIN" IS TO WRITE DOWN YOUR THOUGHTS
IN REAL-TIME AS THEY ARE UNFOLDING.
THIS IS A GREAT MENTAL TOOL TO COUNTER OVER-THINKING
AND TO GET TO THE ROOT OF YOUR WORRIES.
JUST WRITE DOWN WHATEVER POPS INTO YOUR MIND.
DON'T WAIT. DON'T EDIT. DON'T SECOND GUESS.
YOU MIGHT START WITH "I DON'T KNOW WHAT TO WRITE" OR
"I AM HUNGRY". WHATEVER POPS INTO YOUR HEAD IS OK.

DAILY EXERCISE
BRAIN DRAIN

USE THE NEXT PAGE
FOR JOURNALING

SOME HELPFUL QUESTIONS

WHAT AM I
GRATEFUL FOR?

WHAT AM I
ENJOYING LATELY?

WHAT AM I
STRUGGLING
WITH?

WHY RUSH THE PROCESS,
LOOK HOW THE TREES GROW
SLOW & STEADY
THE FUTURE WILL COME
WHEN IT IS READY.

WHICH EMOTIONS ARE
YOU FEELING TODAY ?

WHICH PHYSICAL
SENSATIONS ARE YOU
FEELING TODAY ?

DAILY GRATITUDE

1.

2.

3.

WE ALL WORRY. IT'S NORMAL.
BUT SOMETIMES IT CAN CREATE STRESS AND ANXIETY.

BY WRITING DOWN OUR WORRIES AND WHAT IS
OUT OF CONTROL WE FREE UP MENTAL SPACE.

DAILY EXERCISE

WRITE DOWN THREE THINGS THAT WORRY YOU

1.

2.

3.

WHAT ACTIONS CAN YOU TAKE TO ADDRESS THE THINGS YOU ARE WORRIED ABOUT?

1.

2.

3.

USE THE NEXT PAGE
FOR JOURNALING

SOME HELPFUL QUESTIONS

WHO OR WHAT
MADE ME FEEL
POSITIVE TODAY?

WHAT WORDS
DESCRIBE ME
BEST ?

WHAT INSPIRES
ME ?

DAILY REMINDER

THERE IS A WHOLE OUTSIDE WORLD WITHIN.

WHICH EMOTIONS ARE
YOU FEELING TODAY?

WHICH PHYSICAL
SENSATIONS ARE YOU
FEELING TODAY?

DAILY GRATITUDE

1.

2.

3.

VISUALIZATION

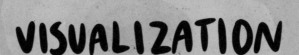

VISUALIZATION IS A CONCEPT
OF IMAGINING A DREAM OR DESIRED
OUTCOME AS IF IT ALREADY HAPPENED.
IT IS A POWERFUL TOOL TO MANIFEST

YOUR GOALS!

VISUALIZE BY DRAWING, WRITING, PASTING PICTURES, OR
ANYTHING ELSE THAT INSPIRES YOU!

USE THE NEXT PAGE FOR JOURNALING

SOME HELPFUL QUESTIONS

WHAT MAKES ME SMILE?

WHAT IS MY FAVORITE WAY TO SPEND THE DAY?

WHAT WOULD MY BODY SAY TO ME RIGHT NOW?

DAILY REMINDER

WHEN THE WORLD
NEEDS IT THE MOST
SHINE YOUR LIGHT

WHICH EMOTIONS ARE YOU FEELING TODAY?

WHICH PHYSICAL SENSATIONS ARE YOU FEELING TODAY?

DAILY GRATITUDE

1.

2.

3.

THE POWER OF WRITING LETTERS

WRITING LETTERS TO YOURSELF
OR TO OTHERS IS A GREAT WAY
TO GAIN NEW INSIGHTS, PROCESS EMOTIONS,
FEEL LESS LONELY, AND DISCOVER DIFFERENT PERSPECTIVES.

WRITE A LETTER TO YOUR PAST SELF

_____
_____
_____
_____
_____
_____
_____
_____
_____
_____
_____
_____
_____
_____
_____
_____
_____
_____
_____
_____
_____
_____
_____

USE THE NEXT PAGE FOR JOURNALING

SOME HELPFUL QUESTIONS

WHICH WORDS WOULD I LIKE TO LIVE BY?

WHAT SCARES ME?

HOW DO I DEAL WITH ANGER?

DAILY REMINDER

LET GO OF THE FEAR,
EMBRACE THE ABUNDANCE AND
LET LIFE REWARD YOUR SPARKLE.

WHICH EMOTIONS ARE
YOU FEELING TODAY?

WHICH PHYSICAL
SENSATIONS ARE YOU
FEELING TODAY?

DAILY GRATITUDE

1.

2.

3.

DAILY EXERCISE

WRITE DOWN THREE AFFIRMATIONS

1.

2.

3.

USE THE NEXT PAGE
FOR JOURNALING

SOME HELPFUL QUESTIONS

HOW DO I WANT
OTHERS TO PERCEIVE
ME?

HOW WOULD I
DESCRIBE
MYSELF?

WHAT WOULD
I LIKE TO CHANGE
ABOUT MY LIFE?

DAILY REMINDER

CHASE WHAT YOU WANT
WITH AN EFFORTLESS GRACE
AND KNOW IT WANTS YOU BACK.

WHICH EMOTIONS ARE
YOU FEELING TODAY ?

WHICH PHYSICAL
SENSATIONS ARE YOU
FEELING TODAY ?

DAILY GRATITUDE

1.

2.

3.

DAILY EXERCISE
BRAIN DRAIN

USE THE NEXT PAGE
FOR JOURNALING

SOME HELPFUL QUESTIONS

WHEN DO I
FEEL MOST
ENERGIZED?

WHICH WORDS
DO I NEED TO
HEAR TODAY?

WHAT IS MY
FAVORITE ACTIVITY?

DAILY REMINDER

I AM GROWING. I AM LEARNING. I AM RISING. I AM SURVIVING. I AM CHANGING. I AM EVOLVING. I AM DREAMING. I AM CREATING. I AM BLOOMING.

WHICH EMOTIONS ARE
YOU FEELING TODAY ?

WHICH PHYSICAL
SENSATIONS ARE YOU
FEELING TODAY ?

DAILY GRATITUDE

1.

2.

3.

DAILY EXERCISE

WRITE DOWN THREE THINGS
THAT WORRY YOU

1.

2.

3.

WHAT ACTIONS CAN YOU TAKE TO ADDRESS THE THINGS YOU ARE WORRIED ABOUT?

1.

2.

3.

USE THE NEXT PAGE
FOR JOURNALING

SOME HELPFUL QUESTIONS

WHAT AM I
LOOKING FORWARD
TO THE MOST?

WHAT IS SOMETHING
NO ONE KNOWS
ABOUT ME?

WHAT IS MY
FAVORITE PLACE?

DAILY REMINDER

FEEL FEEL FEEL FEEL FEEL FEEL FEEL FEEL FEEL FEEL FEEL FEEL FEEL

— DANICA GIM

WHICH EMOTIONS ARE
YOU FEELING TODAY ?

WHICH PHYSICAL
SENSATIONS ARE YOU
FEELING TODAY ?

DAILY GRATITUDE

1.

2.

3.

DAILY EXERCISE

VISUALIZE BY DRAWING, WRITING, PASTING PICTURES OR

ANYTHING ELSE THAT INSPIRES YOU!

USE THE NEXT PAGE
FOR JOURNALING

SOME HELPFUL QUESTIONS

IF I COULD
CHANGE ANYTHING
WHAT WOULD
IT BE?

WHAT CHILDHOOD
MEMORY DO I
REMEMBER?

DO I HAVE
A SECRET?

DAILY REMINDER

WE ARE ALL CONNECTED,
THE PAIN OF THE WORLD
IS OUR OWN.

WHICH EMOTIONS ARE
YOU FEELING TODAY ?

WHICH PHYSICAL
SENSATIONS ARE YOU
FEELING TODAY ?

DAILY GRATITUDE

1.

2.

3.

WRITE A LETTER TO YOUR FUTURE SELF

USE THE NEXT PAGE FOR JOURNALING

SOME HELPFUL QUESTIONS

WHAT IS MY BIGGEST PET PEEVE?

WHAT IS MY HAPPIEST MEMORY?

WHAT IS MY SADDEST MEMORY?

DAILY REMINDER

FOLLOWING
YOUR HEART
IS ALWAYS
WORTH THE
RISK.

WHICH EMOTIONS ARE
YOU FEELING TODAY ?

WHICH PHYSICAL
SENSATIONS ARE YOU
FEELING TODAY ?

DAILY GRATITUDE

1.

2.

3.

DAILY EXERCISE

WRITE DOWN THREE
AFFIRMATIONS

1.

2.

3.

USE THE NEXT PAGE FOR JOURNALING

SOME HELPFUL QUESTIONS

WHAT DO I NEED TODAY?

WHAT DO I NEED TO FORGIVE MYSELF FOR?

WHO DO I WANT TO TALK TO RIGHT NOW?

DAILY
REMINDER

I AM WORTHY
I AM CAPABLE
I AM LOVED

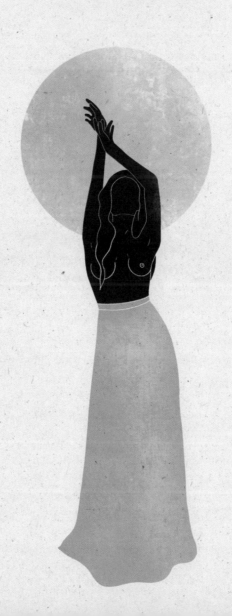

WHICH EMOTIONS ARE
YOU FEELING TODAY?

WHICH PHYSICAL
SENSATIONS ARE YOU
FEELING TODAY?

DAILY GRATITUDE

1.

2.

3.

DAILY EXERCISE
BRAIN DRAIN

_____

_____

_____

_____

_____

_____

_____

_____

_____

_____

_____

_____

_____

_____

_____

_____

_____

_____

_____

_____

_____

_____

USE THE NEXT PAGE FOR JOURNALING

SOME HELPFUL QUESTIONS

WHAT KIND WORDS CAN I SAY TO MYSELF?

WHAT DO I FEEL GUILTY ABOUT?

HOW HAVE I GROWN THE LAST YEAR?

DAILY REMINDER

BE BOLD. BE STRONG.
THIS WILL PASS.

WHICH EMOTIONS ARE
YOU FEELING TODAY?

WHICH PHYSICAL
SENSATIONS ARE YOU
FEELING TODAY?

DAILY GRATITUDE

1.

2.

3.

DAILY EXERCISE

WRITE DOWN THREE THINGS
THAT WORRY YOU

1.

2.

3.

WHAT ACTIONS CAN YOU TAKE TO ADDRESS THE THINGS YOU ARE WORRIED ABOUT?

1.

2.

3.

USE THE NEXT PAGE
FOR JOURNALING

SOME HELPFUL QUESTIONS

WHICH EMOTION
IS MOST DOMINANT
IN ME AT THE MOMENT?

IF I COULD DO
ANYTHING,
WHAT WOULD
IT BE?

WHAT AM I
GOOD AT?

DAILY REMINDER

SOMETIMES ALL YOU NEED IS A NEW PERSPECTIVE.

WHICH EMOTIONS ARE
YOU FEELING TODAY?

WHICH PHYSICAL
SENSATIONS ARE YOU
FEELING TODAY?

DAILY GRATITUDE

1.

2.

3.

VISUALIZE BY DRAWING, WRITING, PASTING PICTURES, OR

ANYTHING ELSE THAT INSPIRES YOU!

USE THE NEXT PAGE
FOR JOURNALING

SOME HELPFUL QUESTIONS

WHAT IS MY
BEST QUALITY?

WHAT COULD
I IMPROVE?

WHAT AM I
MOST AFRAID
OF?

DAILY REMINDER

WHICH EMOTIONS ARE
YOU FEELING TODAY?

WHICH PHYSICAL
SENSATIONS ARE YOU
FEELING TODAY?

DAILY GRATITUDE

1.

2.

3.

DAILY EXERCISE

WRITE A LETTER TO YOUR PARENT(S) / CARE TAKER(S)

_____

_____

_____

_____

_____

_____

_____

_____

_____

_____

_____

_____

_____

_____

_____

_____

_____

_____

_____

_____

_____

USE THE NEXT PAGE FOR JOURNALING

SOME HELPFUL QUESTIONS

WHO IS MY FAVORITE PERSON?

DID I EVER EXPERIENCE SOMETHING THAT STILL FEELS UNRESOLVED TO ME TODAY?

HOW WOULD I DESCRIBE A PERFECT DAY?

DAILY REMINDER

EVERY DAY IS A NEW DAY.

WHICH EMOTIONS ARE
YOU FEELING TODAY ?

WHICH PHYSICAL
SENSATIONS ARE YOU
FEELING TODAY ?

DAILY GRATITUDE

1.

2.

3.

WRITE DOWN THREE
AFFIRMATIONS

1.

2.

3.

USE THE NEXT PAGE FOR JOURNALING

SOME HELPFUL QUESTIONS

HOW DO I WANT OTHERS TO PERCEIVE ME?

HOW WOULD I DESCRIBE MYSELF?

WHAT WOULD I LIKE TO CHANGE ABOUT MY LIFE?

DAILY REMINDER

IS THERE NOT A BEAUTY
IN THE UNKNOWN,
IN KNOWING THAT YOU ARE GROWING
EVEN WHEN YOU ARE FAR AWAY
FROM HOME?

WHICH EMOTIONS ARE
YOU FEELING TODAY ?

WHICH PHYSICAL
SENSATIONS ARE YOU
FEELING TODAY ?

DAILY GRATITUDE

1.

2.

3.

DAILY EXERCISE
BRAIN DRAIN

_____
_____
_____
_____
_____
_____
_____
_____
_____
_____
_____
_____
_____
_____
_____
_____
_____
_____
_____
_____
_____
_____
_____
_____
_____

DON'T STOP UNTIL THE TWO PAGES ARE COMPLETELY FILLED!

USE THE NEXT PAGE
FOR JOURNALING

SOME HELPFUL QUESTIONS

WHOSE BEHAVIOR
MAKES ME
ANXIOUS?
AND WHY?

WHAT IS MY
STRONGEST
BELIEF?

WHAT DID I
DREAM LAST
NIGHT?

DAILY REMINDER

YOU ARE SO MUCH STRONGER
THAN YOU GIVE YOURSELF CREDIT FOR.

WHICH EMOTIONS ARE
YOU FEELING TODAY?

WHICH PHYSICAL
SENSATIONS ARE YOU
FEELING TODAY?

DAILY GRATITUDE

1.

2.

3.

DAILY EXERCISE

WRITE DOWN THREE THINGS
THAT WORRY YOU

1.

2.

3.

WHAT ACTIONS CAN YOU TAKE TO ADDRESS THE THINGS YOU ARE WORRIED ABOUT?

1.

2.

3.

USE THE NEXT PAGE FOR JOURNALING

SOME HELPFUL QUESTIONS

WHICH HABIT CAN I BREAK?

WHAT IS MY VIEW ON SOUL MATES?

HAVE I EVER EXPERIENCED SOMETHING SUPERNATURAL?

DAILY REMINDER

WHICH EMOTIONS ARE
YOU FEELING TODAY ?

WHICH PHYSICAL
SENSATIONS ARE YOU
FEELING TODAY ?

DAILY GRATITUDE

1.

2.

3.

DAILY EXERCISE

VISUALIZE BY DRAWING, WRITING, PASTING PICTURES, OR
ANYTHING ELSE THAT INSPIRES YOU!

USE THE NEXT PAGE FOR JOURNALING

SOME HELPFUL QUESTIONS

WHAT WOULD BE MY PERFECT CAREER?

IN WHICH COUNTRY OTHER THAN MY OWN WOULD I WANT TO LIVE?

IF I COULD GO BACK IN TIME WHAT WOULD I CHANGE?

DAILY
REMINDER

YOU ARE HERE.
YOU MADE IT.

WHICH EMOTIONS ARE
YOU FEELING TODAY ?

WHICH PHYSICAL
SENSATIONS ARE YOU
FEELING TODAY ?

DAILY GRATITUDE

1.

2.

3.

WRITE A LETTER TO A PAST/PRESENT/FUTURE PARTNER

_____
_____
_____
_____
_____
_____
_____
_____
_____
_____
_____
_____
_____
_____
_____
_____
_____
_____
_____
_____
_____
_____
_____
_____

MORE LETTER PROMPT IDEAS

- WRITE A LETTER TO SOMEONE YOU ADMIRE

- WRITE A LETTER TO SOMEONE YOU ARE ANGRY WITH

- WRITE A LETTER TO GOD/ THE UNIVERSE

- WRITE A LETTER TO SOMEONE YOU HAVE WRONGED

- WRITE A LETTER TO SOMEONE YOU NEVER MET

- WRITE A LETTER TO LOVE

- WRITE A LETTER TO YOUR FEAR

- WRITE A LETTER TO A TEACHER IN YOUR LIFE

- WRITE A LETTER TO A CITY YOU WANT TO VISIT

- WRITE A LETTER WITH ADVICE TO YOURSELF

I AM FREE. I AM FREE. I AM FREE. I AM FREE. I AM FREE. I AM FREE. I AM FREE.

USE THE NEXT PAGE FOR JOURNALING

SOME HELPFUL QUESTIONS

WHO DO I MISS?

WHAT IS MY VIEW ON RELIGION?

IF I WON THE LOTTERY, WHAT WOULD I DO?

MORE SPACE
FOR
WRITING

DANICA GIM is a European writer and artist currently residing in the Netherlands. Art Nouveau and black-figure style heavily inspire her style. In 2017 she started sharing her poetry and art on Instagram, where she has since amassed a large and diverse international audience. When Danica is not writing or making art, she is committed to raising awareness for Endometriosis.

danicagim.com
instagram.com/danica.gim